TO:

FROM:

DATE:

ENCOURAGEMENT *from*

A PLACE CALLED
HEAVEN

Words of Hope about
Your Eternal Home

DR. ROBERT
JEFFRESS

BakerBooks

a division of Baker Publishing Group
Grand Rapids, Michigan

© 2022 by Robert Jeffress

Published by Baker Books
a division of Baker Publishing Group
PO Box 6287, Grand Rapids, MI 49516-6287
www.bakerbooks.com

Printed in the United States of America

ISBN 978-1-5409-0176-7 (cloth)
ISBN 978-1-4934-3408-4 (ebook)

Content in this book has been adapted from Robert Jeffress, *A Place Called Heaven: 10 Surprising Truths about Your Eternal Home* (Grand Rapids: Baker Books, 2017) and Robert Jeffress, *A Place Called Heaven Devotional: 100 Days of Living in the Hope of Eternity* (Grand Rapids: Baker Books, 2021).

Unless otherwise indicated, Scripture quotations are from the (NASB®) New American Standard Bible®, Copyright © 1960, 1971, 1977, 1995 by The Lockman Foundation. Used by permission. All rights reserved. www.lockman.org

Scripture quotations labeled NIV are from THE HOLY BIBLE, NEW INTERNATIONAL VERSION®, NIV® Copyright © 1973, 1978, 1984, 2011 by Biblica, Inc.® Used by permission. All rights reserved worldwide.

Scripture quotations labeled NLT are from the *Holy Bible*, New Living Translation, copyright © 1996, 2004, 2007, 2013, 2015 by Tyndale House Foundation. Used by permission of Tyndale House Publishers, Inc., Carol Stream, Illinois 60188. All rights reserved.

All italics in Scripture quotations are the author's emphasis.

Published in association with Yates & Yates, www.yates2.com.

Baker Publishing Group publications use paper produced from sustainable forestry practices and post-consumer waste whenever possible.

22 23 24 25 26 27 28   7 6 5 4 3 2 1

Keep seeking the things above, where Christ is, seated at the right hand of God. Set your mind on the things above, not on the things that are on earth.

—Colossians 3:1–2

Contents

*We all long
for our eternal home—
that "place called heaven."*

CHAPTER 1

What Difference Does a Future Heaven Make in My Life Today?

Most Christians don't spend a lot of time thinking about heaven. That's understandable. The overwhelming responsibilities of this world often eclipse much thought about the next world. Heaven seems remote and irrelevant to our existence.

Yet we all yearn for a better world, especially when we experience disappointments, such as a bad report from the doctor, the betrayal of a friend, the breakup of an intimate relationship, a job loss or financial hardship, or the death of a loved one. At those times we want to believe—we *have* to believe—that there is a better place.

Heaven is not some fanciful, imaginary destination created by well-intentioned individuals to dull the pain of this world and keep us from being overwhelmed by the harsh realities of life. Over and over in the Bible, God promised that His people will live with Him forever in a place where perfect righteousness dwells.

Jesus Christ Himself—the One whom Christians are banking on for their eternal destiny—assured us that heaven is a real place. In the Sermon on the Mount, Jesus said, "He who does the will of My Father who is in heaven will enter" (Matt. 7:21).

Behold, I create new
heavens and a new earth;
and the former things will not be
remembered or come to mind.
—Isaiah 65:17

For those of us who are Christians, this one-way trip that will last for eternity is to that "place called heaven."

Wise travelers go through a routine to prepare for leaving on a vacation. They put a hold on their mail, check the weather to know what to pack, and make sure they have a ticket. How much more important is it for us to prepare for our ultimate journey to our eternal home?

The Bible says every one of us will someday make a trip to a place that is mostly unfamiliar to us. And this destination won't be a brief vacation; it will be an eternal destination. For those of us who are Christians, this one-way trip that will last for eternity is to that "place called heaven."

Throughout the Bible, we see that God has ordained every day of our lives. "A person's days are determined," Job said; God "decreed the number of his months and . . . set limits he cannot exceed" (Job 14:5 NIV). Run all the miles you can and eat all the bran muffins you want; you're not going to live on earth one second longer than God has predetermined.

The psalmist declared, "My times are in Your hand" (Ps. 31:15). Even Jesus's death occurred according to "the predetermined plan and foreknowledge of God" (Acts 2:23).

Just as the day of Jesus's death was determined by God, so is the day of your death. That's a great reason to reflect on your eternal home.

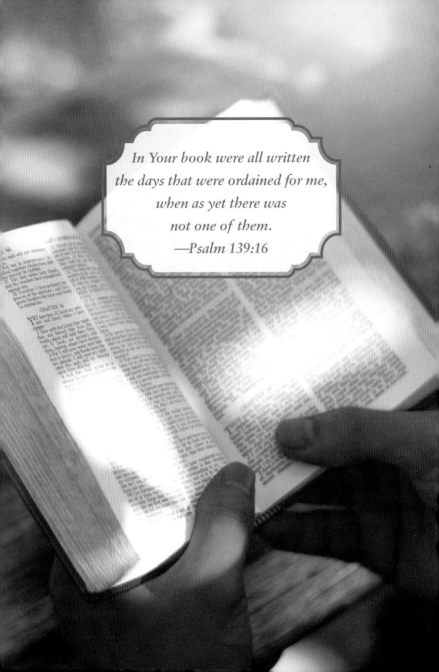

In Your book were all written
the days that were ordained for me,
when as yet there was
not one of them.
—Psalm 139:16

The more we think about the next world, the more effective we become in this world.

The realization that we are headed to heaven should motivate us to spend our limited time on earth productively. No need to be concerned about piling up money—we'll leave it all behind when we depart. No reason to worry about what other people think about us—our calling to our new location is assured. Instead, grasping the reality of the "place called heaven" that awaits us should liberate us to invest our few remaining years on earth as wisely as possible.

The more we think about the next world, the more effective we become in this world.

For followers of Jesus Christ, death is like moving from the frozen tundra of the arctic circle to the sun-kissed beaches of Hawaii. The apostle Paul described a Christian's change of location at death like this: being "absent from the body" means being "at home with the Lord" (2 Cor. 5:8).

Paul struggled between two desires: to depart for heaven as soon as possible and to remain on earth to fulfill his ministry. He realized that every minute spent alive on earth was a minute away from the home Jesus had prepared for him in heaven. We were made for heaven, not earth.

We were made
for heaven, not earth.

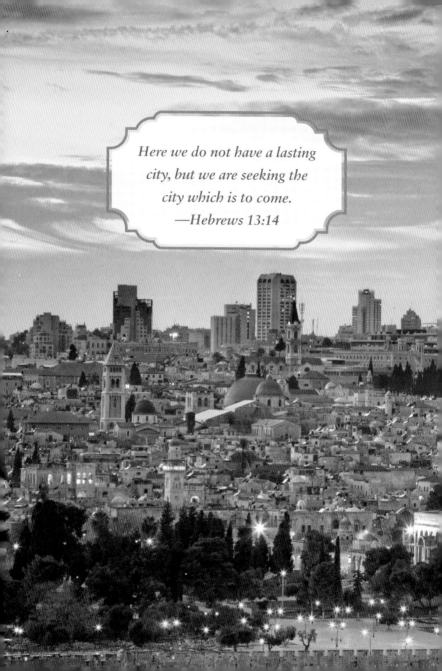

Here we do not have a lasting city, but we are seeking the city which is to come.
—Hebrews 13:14

God doesn't tell us everything we want to know about our future home. Instead, the Bible gives us a pencil sketch of heaven. Why doesn't God tell us more about our eternal home?

Our minds are incapable of fully comprehending the magnificence of heaven. For example, how could you adequately describe a beautiful sunset to the blind or convey the majesty of a symphony to the deaf? Our minds are incapable of processing the realities of the next world.

Additionally, if God told us *everything* about heaven, we would find it difficult to focus on the assignments He has charged us with on earth. That's why God has given us just enough information about heaven to whet our appetite for our glorious future that is yet to come.

People often ask, "Why does God allow suffering and evil in the world?" God has given us the promise of heaven to put suffering in perspective.

You may be experiencing a difficulty you think will never end. You pray, "God, why don't You stop this?" He understands what you are going through. Whatever problem you are facing is real, and it is heavy to you. Yet the difficulties you experience in this life are light when compared to the future God is preparing for you in heaven.

Focusing on the hope of heaven doesn't eliminate suffering, but it does help us put our suffering in perspective.

Focusing on the hope of heaven doesn't eliminate suffering, but it does help us put our suffering in perspective.

This Jesus, who has been taken up from you into heaven, will come in just the same way as you have watched Him go into heaven.

—Acts 1:11

CHAPTER 2

Is Heaven a Real Place or Is It a State of Mind?

Atheists sometimes accuse Christians of living in a fantasyland—of looking forward to a heaven that isn't real. "If it can't be proven scientifically that heaven exists, then it must not exist," they argue.

Where do we go to find out if heaven is a real place or a figment of our imaginations? If heaven is where God dwells, then we can assume God is the one true expert on the subject. Therefore, if we want to know whether heaven is real or simply a state of mind, we should turn to God's Book, the Bible, to answer that question.

Since the Bible is the inspired truth from God, Scripture is the place we turn to find out whether heaven is a real place or a state of mind.

As Jesus talked of His impending death, His disciples wondered, *Will we ever see Jesus again?* Jesus reassured them that He would return and take them to heaven—to the "Father's house."

Jesus said, "I *go to prepare* a place for you" (John 14:2). The act of going and preparing speaks to something tangible. And His words "place" and "dwelling" describe a real, geographical location.

Jesus is in heaven right now overseeing the greatest construction project in history—our heavenly home. And if He is creating an elaborate home for us, we can be sure He will return to escort us into that indescribable, new destination He is preparing for us.

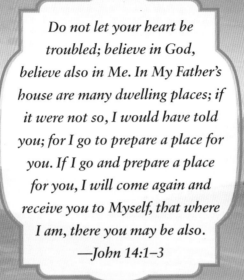

Do not let your heart be troubled; believe in God, believe also in Me. In My Father's house are many dwelling places; if it were not so, I would have told you; for I go to prepare a place for you. If I go and prepare a place for you, I will come again and receive you to Myself, that where I am, there you may be also.

—John 14:1–3

*Jesus was saying,
"Do you want to get to
heaven? Follow Me."*

Where is heaven? Can you locate it on a map? Thomas asked Jesus, "We do not know where You are going, how do we know the way?" (John 14:5). That is a logical question. Jesus told them they were going to the Father's house—where was that? And how would they get there?

Jesus helped the disciples recalibrate their spiritual GPS. Since they wanted to know how to get to heaven, Jesus said, "I am the way, and the truth, and the life; no one comes to the Father but through Me" (v. 6). In other words, Jesus was saying, "Do you want to get to heaven? Follow Me."

Does heaven exist in time and space, or is it a realm we can't access from earth? To answer that question, we need to distinguish between the present heaven where God resides and the future heaven Jesus is constructing for us.

The present heaven is where Christians go immediately when they die to enjoy the presence of the Lord. Paul described it in 2 Corinthians 5:8: "To be absent from the body [is] to be at home with the Lord." The future heaven is where believers will someday spend eternity, and it is still under construction. It is the "place" Jesus is preparing for us (John 14:2).

The present heaven is where Christians go immediately when they die to enjoy the presence of the Lord.

I saw a new heaven and
a new earth; for the
first heaven and the first
earth passed away.
—Revelation 21:1

The Bible refers to three heavens. The *first heaven* is earth's atmosphere—the air we breathe and the space where birds fly. The *second heaven* is outer space—the planets, stars, and galaxies. The *third heaven* represents the presence of God—where Christians immediately go when they die. It is sometimes called Paradise.

But there is also a *fourth heaven*—the future heaven God is preparing for us right now. This is the place of our future and forever home. This fourth heaven includes the "new heaven" and "new earth" John described in Revelation 21–22. The fourth heaven will literally be heaven on earth. This future heaven is the place where all believers will live for eternity.

We won't go up to heaven and leave this earth behind forever. Instead, God will bring the new heaven down to a newly created earth. This new earth—like the old one—will be *physical* (Rev. 21). Resurrected believers with physically transformed bodies require a physical home. And God will create such a place for us.

The new earth will also be *familiar*. Heaven—the new earth—won't be like moving to a foreign country. In many ways, this new earth will resemble our present earth but be vastly improved. Those who live on the new earth will experience fellowship with God and one another in joyous, loving relationships untainted by sin.

[God] will wipe away every tear from their eyes; and there will no longer be any death; there will no longer be any mourning, or crying, or pain; the first things have passed away.
—Revelation 21:4

What we do on earth
today reverberates in the
halls of heaven forever.

Heaven is the promise that God will eventually make all things right and fulfill our deepest longings. Although God's promise is yet future, it should make a tremendous difference in our lives today. This is the hope of heaven—that *all* of creation will receive what it has long desired: freedom from the crushing oppression of sin.

How we wait for this "place called heaven"—whether with anticipation or anxiety, whether with focused or unfocused living—matters both now and in the future. For what we do on earth today reverberates in the halls of heaven forever.

He has also set eternity
in [our] heart.
—*Ecclesiastes 3:11*

Have Some People Already Visited Heaven?

Have some people who are alive right now already visited heaven? Several bestsellers have been written by people who claim, "We went to the other side, and we've come back to tell you about it."

Why are we fascinated by near-death experiences? Deep inside each of us is a longing for heaven. While there is much to love about earth, we instinctively know there must be something more, something better that awaits us on the other side of death.

God has "set eternity in [our] heart" (Eccles. 3:11), meaning we desire to know what God is preparing for us after we leave this earth. We know there is more to life than what we are experiencing right now.

You may not have had a near-death experience, but chances are some illness or close call has brought your mortality into sharper focus. Coming face-to-face with the prospect of death—whether your own or that of someone you love—can be jolting. Such an experience is a stark reminder of the brevity of life . . . and the length of eternity. So it makes sense that those who have "died" and experienced the sensation of traveling to another world would never be the same after they "return" to life on this side of the grave.

However, just because someone has had a near-death experience doesn't mean his or her experience is real.

It is appointed for men to die once and after this comes judgment.
—Hebrews 9:27

*The Bible is sufficient
because the Bible is true.*

In the Bible, God has provided us with a wealth of information about the future that awaits us after death. Although God hasn't told us everything we may *want* to know, He has revealed everything we *need* to know.

The Bible is sufficient because the Bible is true. And when it comes to evaluating near-death experiences, we must test all claims against its teaching. To do so fulfills John's command to "not believe every spirit, but test the spirits to see whether they are from God" (1 John 4:1), like the wise Bereans who examined the Scriptures carefully to see whether Paul's preaching was true (Acts 17:11).

Are near-death experiences valid? Adding to or taking away from the Bible is condemned by God (Rev. 22:18–19). Anyone who says, "God has given me a new revelation about heaven" is treading on dangerous ground.

We should also question the identity of any being of light. Many people who had a near-death experience claim to have met angels or even Jesus. Yet we need to be careful of any so-called being of light who gives a message that contradicts Scripture. Hebrews 13:8 says, "Jesus Christ is the same yesterday and today and forever." The Jesus in heaven does not contradict what Jesus said on earth. Jesus said there is one way to heaven, and it is through faith in Him.

Jesus Christ is the same yesterday and today and forever.
—Hebrews 13:8

*Everything we need to know
about our eternal home
is found in the Bible.*

We need to take seriously the warning of 1 Timothy 4:1: "In later times some will fall away from the faith, paying attention to deceitful spirits and doctrines of demons."

I believe some near-death experiences are demonic. When people say they saw a light and a divine being telling them that everyone is going to heaven, I believe them—but the bright light they saw was not God. In 2 Corinthians 11:14, Paul said, "Satan disguises himself as an angel of light." He deceives people about what awaits them on the other side.

God can do whatever He wants to do, but the weight of evidence is against near-death experiences. Everything we need to know about our eternal home is found in the Bible.

The presupposition behind books about near-death experiences is this: "The Bible is good, but not sufficient. God has given me more information about heaven to share with you for $22.95."

Paul said, "We do not want you to be uninformed, brethren, about those who are asleep [Christians who have died], so that you will not grieve as do the rest who have no hope. For if we believe that Jesus died and rose again, even so God will bring with Him those who have fallen asleep in Jesus" (1 Thess. 4:13–14).

Every time I read those verses to those who have lost a loved one, God's Word comforts them. That is the power of God's Word. The Bible is sufficient. We don't need any extrabiblical revelation about heaven.

*All Scripture is inspired by God
and profitable for teaching,
for reproof, for correction, for
training in righteousness; so that
the man of God may be adequate,
equipped for every good work.*
—2 Timothy 3:16–17

*What's in store for us is
so magnificent that human
words only diminish
the glory of heaven.*

The Bible does not record any near-death experiences. There are biblical accounts of God raising people from the dead, but none of them told what they saw on the other side. Even the apostle Paul, who wrote much of the New Testament, said he "was caught up to the third heaven" but was "not permitted to speak" about his experience (2 Cor. 12:2, 4).

Why has God restricted the information we have about heaven? What's in store for us is so magnificent that human words only diminish the glory of heaven. And if we knew what was awaiting us, we couldn't wait to get out of here! That's why Paul, who had seen heaven, was able to say, "To live is Christ and to die is gain" (Phil. 1:21).

There is one fate,
but there are two
different destinations:
heaven and hell.

CHAPTER 4

Do Christians Immediately Go to Heaven When They Die?

While there are certain things about the afterlife we cannot know for sure, one thing is clear: we are all going to die one day. As the old adage says, "No one gets out of this world alive."

Why is death inevitable for every person? In Ecclesiastes 9:2, Solomon said, "It is the same for all. There is one fate for the righteous and for the wicked." It does not matter whether you are good or bad, righteous or unrighteous, a believer or an unbeliever; there is one fate for everybody: death. We are all going to die. There is one fate, but there are two different destinations: heaven and hell.

Death is every person's fate because every man, woman, and child is guilty of sin against God. We have all inherited the virus of sin. Romans 3:23 says, "All have sinned and fall short of the glory of God." And sin is punishable by death: "For the wages of sin is death" (6:23).

From the beginning, death was the just punishment for sin. God warned Adam and Eve that if they rebelled against His clear command, they would die. And die they did. With the exceptions of Enoch and Elijah (and believers alive at the rapture of the church), every person since Adam and Eve has died or will die.

The wages of sin is death.
—Romans 6:23

For a Christian, death is not the end. It's the beginning of our eternal reunion with God.

What happens to Christians when we die? Do we cease to exist? Do we go to sleep, awaiting our resurrection? Do we go into a waiting place, hoping somebody will pray hard enough or give enough money to get us out?

The thought of death can fill us with dread. However, knowing our destination when we depart this life can dramatically diminish that fear. One of my mentors used to say, "We are not in the land of the living headed to the land of the dying. Instead, we are in the land of the dying on our way to the land of the living." For a Christian, death is not the end. It's the beginning of our eternal reunion with God.

The moment Christians die, we immediately depart from this world into the presence of God. In Luke 23:43, Jesus said to the thief on the cross who professed faith, "Today you shall be with Me in Paradise." And in Acts 7:59, Stephen said, "Lord Jesus, receive my spirit!"

In 2 Corinthians 5:6, Paul explained, "While we are at home in the body we are absent from the Lord." We cannot be in two locations at once. We often think this world is our home, but it's not. Yes, we have people we love here. Yes, God has given us an assignment here. But it is temporary. As long as we are here, we cannot also be at home in heaven with God.

As long as we are here, we cannot also be at home in heaven with God.

We are of good courage, I say, and prefer rather to be absent from the body and to be at home with the Lord.
—2 Corinthians 5:8

At the rapture, all Christians will receive glorified bodies in which they will live for eternity. In 1 Thessalonians 4:16, Paul said, "The Lord Himself will descend from heaven with a shout . . . and the dead in Christ will rise first." The "dead in Christ" are Christians who have already died. Their spirits are in heaven and, at the rapture, their bodies will be raised. Believers who are alive at that time will also be caught up, and together they will "meet the Lord in the air" (v. 17).

In 1 Corinthians 15:52, Paul said at that moment, "in the twinkling of an eye . . . the dead will be raised imperishable, and we will be changed." Christians will receive brand-new bodies that are free from suffering and death.

What happened to Old Testament saints who died before Jesus came? Where did they go when they died?

People in the Old Testament were saved the same way you and I are saved: by the death of Jesus Christ on the cross for their sins. Genesis 15:6 says Abraham "believed in the LORD; and He reckoned it to him as righteousness." Abraham and other Old Testament saints believed what God revealed to them, and their faith allowed them to be saved on credit. The bill for their sins, just like the bill for our sins, was paid in full at the cross. That's why Jesus said, "It is finished!" (John 19:30).

All believers—whether they lived before Christ or after Christ—are saved the same way: by the death of Jesus Christ.

All believers—whether they lived before Christ or after Christ—are saved the same way: by the death of Jesus Christ.

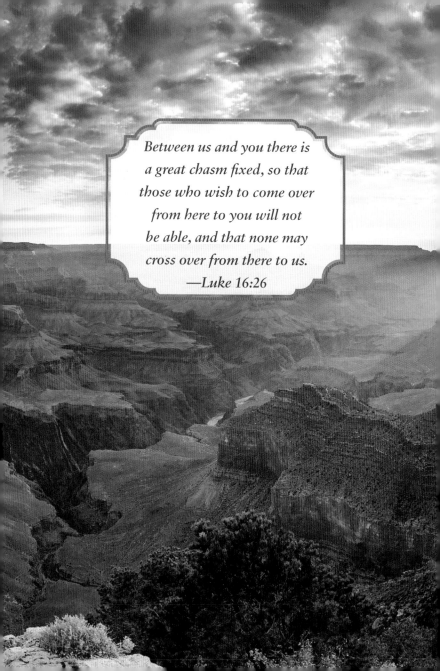

Between us and you there is a great chasm fixed, so that those who wish to come over from here to you will not be able, and that none may cross over from there to us.
—Luke 16:26

When we die, we immediately begin experiencing God's blessing or God's judgment. In His story of the rich man and Lazarus, Jesus taught that God has established an impenetrable barrier between the righteous and unrighteous—"a great chasm fixed" (Luke 16:26)—preventing those in heaven to travel to Hades and those in Hades to travel to heaven, thereby eliminating any possibility of salvation after death.

The moment we die, our eternal destiny is sealed—forever. If you wait until you die to choose your destination, then you will have waited one second too long. Heaven and hell are eternal choices.

In heaven, everything will be
eternally good, beautiful,
enjoyable, refreshing,
fascinating, and exciting.

CHAPTER 5

What Will We Do in Heaven?

Many people think heaven will be boring. But nothing could be further from the truth! People who believe heaven is boring have a flawed understanding of Satan and God.

Have you ever been seated at a dinner party next to a boring person? Minutes seem like hours, and it feels like the evening will never end. Satan is that kind of companion. There's nothing interesting about him. He has never created anything in his entire existence. Who would want to be stuck with him for eternity?

But God is exceedingly fascinating: just look at the world He created for us to live in! In heaven, everything will be eternally good, beautiful, enjoyable, fascinating, and exciting because heaven's Creator is all those things.

When God created Adam, He gave him two primary responsibilities: to work and to worship. Scripture says God "placed the man whom He had formed" in the garden of Eden "to cultivate it and keep it" (Gen. 2:8, 15). That was the work Adam was to accomplish.

But Adam was also created to worship God. Adam and Eve had daily fellowship with the Lord—they walked with Him "in the cool of the day" (Gen. 3:8). When Christ establishes our eternal home, it will be an Eden-like existence. And just as Adam had two primary responsibilities in Eden, we will have two primary responsibilities in heaven.

The LORD God took the man
and put him into the garden of
Eden to cultivate it and keep it.
—Genesis 2:15

One day we will add our voices to that heavenly chorus of angels, shouting, "Hallelujah!"

What will our worship be like in heaven? The angels ceaselessly worship the Lord with shouts of praise. Isaiah said, "The foundations of the thresholds trembled" when the angels worshiped in heaven (Isa. 6:4). One day we will add our voices to that heavenly chorus of angels, shouting, "Hallelujah!"

But there's more to our heavenly worship than size and volume. In heaven, no one will merely go through the motions of worship; worship in heaven will be spontaneous, genuine, and exhilarating. This kind of worship that flows out of the deepest recesses of our hearts will happen every time we are in God's presence in the new heaven and new earth.

While worshiping God will be a central activity in heaven, it will not be our only activity. Just as Christians today can praise God while engaging in other tasks throughout the week, Christians in heaven will worship God during designated times as well as while involved in other activities.

Worship is a continual awareness of, gratitude toward, and submission to God in everything we do. God is honored with our worship while we're enjoying a delicious dinner, sitting on a beach reflecting on His majestic power, or even preparing for a difficult conversation. We must quit thinking that we can only worship God while doing *nothing* else. Rather, we worship while doing *everything* else.

Whether, then, you eat or drink or whatever you do, do all to the glory of God.
—1 Corinthians 10:31

In heaven, we will experience the work that God intended for us to enjoy.

Since our lives in heaven are extensions of our lives now, we shouldn't be surprised that God plans for us to continue working in heaven. You and I were created in the image of God, so we were created to be workers.

We may wince at the concept of working for eternity because our labor on earth has been burdened by the effects of sin's curse. But in heaven, all those effects will evaporate because "there will no longer be any curse" (Rev. 22:3). In this world, work—no matter how much we enjoy it—can be exhausting. In the new world, work will be exhilarating.

In heaven, we will experience the work that God intended for us to enjoy.

Heaven will be a time of enjoying other believers. God made us in such a way that we need fellowship with others, and in heaven we will enjoy that in a perfect way. Think about how fascinating it will be to talk with your great-great-grandparents in heaven. Imagine what it will be like to hear Noah talk about building the ark, David recount his victory over Goliath, or Mary Magdalene describe the first Easter morning. Think about talking theology with Martin Luther, science with Blaise Pascal, or music with Fanny Crosby.

From our first day in heaven, and every day thereafter, we will walk the streets of the new heaven and new earth and enjoy perfect fellowship with one another.

Many will come from east
and west, and recline at the table
with Abraham, Isaac and Jacob
in the kingdom of heaven.
—Matthew 8:11

We *will have all eternity*
to get to know the Lord.

Heaven will be a time of learning more about God. The Old Testament prophet Habakkuk said, "The earth will be filled with the knowledge of the glory of the LORD" (2:14). But have you ever wondered how that knowledge will come? When we die, is there a sudden information dump into our brains where we know everything about God? Maybe.

But think about your most important relationships on earth. Hasn't part of the enjoyment of that relationship been learning more and more about that person over a period of time rather than learning everything at once? There is joy in discovery. I think we will have all eternity to get to know the Lord.

When God created the world, He rested on the seventh day, not because He was exhausted but to reflect on what He had accomplished. God also designated times for the Israelites to rest.

I think that in heaven, there will be times we will rest from our labors, times we will be able to enjoy true satisfaction in a job well done. Rest reminds us that as important as our work is, there is more to life than working.

Heaven will be a place of enjoying the perfect fellowship with others and perfect relationship with God we have always longed for. Aren't you ready to go? God has a great, indescribable future planned for those who love Him.

Come to Me, all who are weary and heavy-laden, and I will give you rest.
—Matthew 11:28

There are some passages
in the Bible that indicate
people in heaven know what
is happening on earth.

CHAPTER 6

Do People in Heaven Know What Is Happening on Earth?

Can residents of heaven watch what is taking place on earth? If so, could they be watching you right now?

There are some passages in the Bible that indicate people in heaven know what is happening on earth. For example, Christ is aware of the obedience and disobedience of Christians on earth, since He condemned and commended the seven churches in Revelation 2–3. Furthermore, the apostle Paul realized that a heavenly audience was witnessing his actions on earth, since he described his life as "a spectacle to the world, both to angels and to men" (1 Cor. 4:9). We can assume from this verse that angels are aware of the activities of people on earth.

Hebrews 12:1 appears to imply that the occupants of heaven are like spectators at a track meet, sitting in the stands watching us run the race of faith. If we're honest, it's creepy to think of a billion eyes observing you. Do you really want people in heaven to be watching your every move?

That's not what Hebrews 12:1 teaches. In context, the "cloud of witnesses" refers to the Old Testament saints mentioned in Hebrews 11. The writer was saying that in light of the examples of those who persevered in faith, we should also obey God regardless of the obstacles we face.

Nevertheless, there is some indication that those in heaven are aware of what takes place outside of heaven.

Since we have so great a cloud of witnesses surrounding us, let us also lay aside every encumbrance and the sin which so easily entangles us, and let us run with endurance the race that is set before us.

—Hebrews 12:1

The residents of heaven are aware of what is happening on earth.

During the future time of God's judgment on the earth known as the tribulation, many will come to faith in Jesus. However, these tribulation saints will pay the ultimate price for following Christ. In Revelation, John saw these martyred believers around God's throne, crying out for justice (Rev. 6:9–10). These Christ-followers in heaven were aware of what was happening on earth.

Later in John's vision, at the end of the tribulation, the saints of heaven rose up with a great roar of approval over God's judgment on earth. Again, the praise of believers in heaven for God's judgment against His enemies on the earth is possible only if the residents of heaven are aware of what is happening on earth.

Jesus said, "There will be more joy in heaven over one sinner who repents than over ninety-nine righteous persons who need no repentance. . . . There is joy in the presence of the angels of God over one sinner who repents" (Luke 15:7, 10).

Notice that Jesus didn't say angels rejoiced, though they probably do. He said rejoicing took place in heaven "in the *presence* of the angels," indicating that Christians in heaven are celebrating the salvation of sinners on earth.

If citizens of heaven rejoice at the salvation of sinners, then they not only know what is taking place on earth in a general sense but are aware of specific choices individuals are making on earth—whether they have accepted or rejected Christ's offer of salvation.

Christians in heaven are celebrating the salvation of sinners on earth.

Fixing our eyes on Jesus, the author and perfecter of faith, who for the joy set before Him endured the cross, despising the shame, and has sat down at the right hand of the throne of God.
—Hebrews 12:2

Will the joy of heaven be diminished by what happens on earth? How can we be happy in heaven while watching those we care about on earth suffering from devastating illnesses, broken relationships, or destructive addictions?

Some people say, "We'll be so caught up with the joys of heaven that we won't be aware of what is happening on earth." Other people think the only reason we are able to enjoy life despite the suffering of others is that we are not like Jesus.

Though Jesus wept over the unsaved when He was on earth, Scripture indicates He is experiencing unending joy in heaven. Hebrews 12:2 says Jesus endured the cross so He could experience "the joy set before Him." Jesus suffered on earth so He could experience joy in heaven, and the same is true for us.

Psalm 16:11 describes what it will be like when we are in the presence of the Lord: "In Your presence is fullness of joy; in Your right hand there are pleasures forever." When we are in heaven, we will experience unending pleasure and joy.

In heaven, we will fully understand the plan and the justice of God. When we see Jesus in all His glory, we will understand His holiness and His retribution against those who refuse to accept the gospel. Nothing that happens on earth or in hell will diminish in the slightest degree the unending joy God has planned for us in heaven.

In heaven, we will fully understand the plan and the justice of God.

God *causes all things to work
together for good to those who
love God, to those who are
called according to His purpose.*
—Romans 8:28

God has designed our lives on earth like a tapestry. Some lives are twisted, knotted, or cut short. Other lives are of impressive length and color. Why? Not because one thread is more important than another thread, but because God's tapestry requires it.

Only from the perspective of heaven will we be able to see the right side of God's plan for our lives and understand how He is working all things "together for good" (Rom. 8:28). The tangled mess of broken relationships, catastrophic accidents, and sudden deaths that make no sense to those of us trapped in time and space on earth will be viewed completely differently from the perspective of heaven.

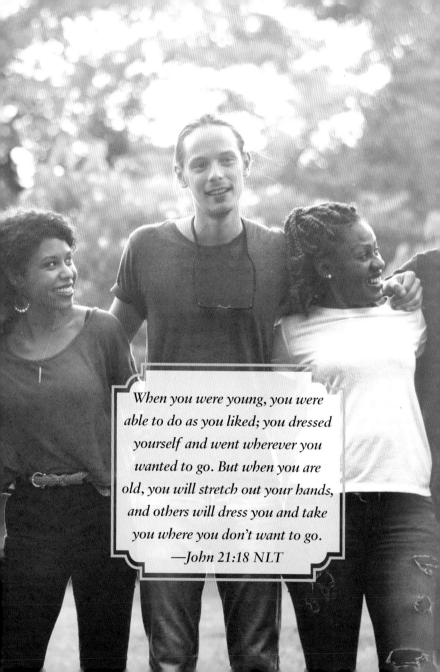

When you were young, you were able to do as you liked; you dressed yourself and went wherever you wanted to go. But when you are old, you will stretch out your hands, and others will dress you and take you where you don't want to go.

—John 21:18 NLT

CHAPTER 7

Will We Know One Another in Heaven?

For those of us of a certain age, it's unnerving to look in a full-length mirror. Most people don't age gracefully. Hearing loss, fading eyesight, and creaking joints accompany our advancing years. If and when we get to old age, we'll hardly recognize ourselves.

When it comes to the next life, we are curious about who we will be in heaven. Will we be ourselves? And if so, which self—the young, energetic go-getter or the old, lethargic individual with hardly enough get up to go? Will we recognize loved ones, and will they recognize us—and which version of "us" will they know? When we get to heaven, what will our bodies be like? To find answers, we need to understand Jesus's promise of a resurrection body.

In heaven, we are not going to be spirits floating around. We are going to have physical bodies. That should not be a surprise when we remember that God's original design for us was both a spirit and a body. Genesis 2:7 says, "The LORD God formed man of dust from the ground, and breathed into his nostrils the breath of life; and man became a living being."

Just as we possess physical bodies in this world, we will also exist and relate to one another in physical bodies in the next world. God's future plan for us includes a physical resurrection. Believers will receive new, resurrection bodies that are necessary to experience God's unending blessing.

Believers will receive new, resurrection bodies that are necessary to experience God's unending blessing.

Blessed and holy is the one who has a part in the first resurrection; over these the second death has no power.
—Revelation 20:6

The Bible talks about two resurrections. The resurrection for Christians is called the *first resurrection*. The first resurrection doesn't refer to a point in time; it refers to the people who will receive a new body to experience God's blessing. All believers are part of the first resurrection, the resurrection of the saved.

The *second resurrection* is the resurrection of all the unsaved. One day, every unbeliever ever born will be raised from the dead. The second resurrection occurs before the great white throne judgment (Rev. 20:13). These unbelievers rejected the grace of God. And as good as their works may be, no one is good enough to inherit heaven.

Everyone, believers and unbelievers, will receive a new body for all eternity.

How can the bodies of people who have died come to life again? In 1 Corinthians 15:36, the apostle Paul described our resurrection using the analogy of planting and harvesting: "That which you sow does not come to life unless it dies." Death is necessary for there to be a future harvest.

Paul explained why in verse 50: "Flesh and blood cannot inherit the kingdom of God; nor does the perishable inherit the imperishable." Think of it this way: your body is perfectly designed for this world, but it is not suitable for living on Mars. It is the same way in terms of this earth and the new heaven and new earth.

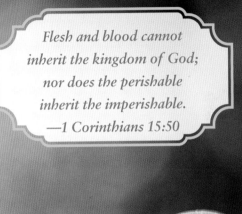

Flesh and blood cannot
inherit the kingdom of God;
nor does the perishable
inherit the imperishable.
—1 Corinthians 15:50

We should not view death
as the end of something
great but as the beginning
of something greater.

In 1 Corinthians 15, Paul explained that when we die, our bodies are like seeds that are planted in the ground, so to speak, so that something better can be harvested later. We should not view death as the end of something great but as the beginning of something greater.

We are not going to carry our old bodies into heaven. Aren't you grateful for that? Our old bodies are raised, but then they are completely renovated. And what we will receive from God is far superior to what was planted. We will not get a body that is totally dissimilar to what we were. Our new bodies are going to resemble our old bodies.

In heaven, our bodies will be perfect. No more cancer. No more heart attacks. No more strokes. Revelation 21:4 says, "The first things have passed away." And Revelation 22:3 says, "There will no longer be any curse."

In heaven, our bodies will be personal. When we are raised from the dead, we do not become somebody else. We are still ourselves. In 1 John 3:2, John said, "We will be like [Jesus]." That does not mean we all become mini-Christs without any distinction. It means we inherit heavenly DNA like Jesus but retain our own identities.

In your resurrection body, you will be you. You will not be someone else.

We know that when [Jesus] appears, we will be like Him, because we will see Him just as He is.
—1 John 3:2

In heaven, you will become the you God intended you to be.

Your body, your talents, your passions, and your spirit are what make you *you*. In heaven, these will be perfected and glorified, but you won't become an angel or someone else. In heaven, you will become the *you* God intended you to be.

When we get to heaven, we'll recognize one another. We'll even recognize saints we've never seen before, as Peter, James, and John recognized Moses and Elijah when they appeared with Jesus at His transfiguration (Matt. 17:4).

The relationships we formed on earth will continue in heaven. But there will be no arguments, envy, or misunderstandings. In heaven, all things are made new. That is something truly to look forward to in that "place called heaven."

Making it to heaven is the goal,
but hearing Jesus say, "Well done,
good and faithful servant!" is
the key to ultimate victory.

CHAPTER 8

Will Heaven Be the Same for Everyone?

I n a football game, making it to the end zone is the goal, but making it to the right end zone is imperative for winning. It is the same way in the Christian life. Making it to heaven is the goal, but hearing Jesus say, "Well done, good and faithful servant!" (Matt. 25:21 NIV) is the key to ultimate victory. Some Christians will be celebrated by God for the way they played the game. Other Christians will be evaluated by God for doing little to contribute to the success of the team.

When "we . . . all stand before the judgment seat of God" (Rom. 14:10), some will receive great rewards and others won't. It's a hard but inescapable truth: heaven will not be the same for every Christian.

No one escapes God's judgment. However, there is not one single judgment for all humankind. Instead, unbelievers will stand before Christ at the great white throne judgment. This judgment of unbelievers will occur at the end of the millennial kingdom, resulting in condemnation (Rev. 20:11–15).

But believers will appear before a very different judgment, called "the judgment seat of Christ" (2 Cor. 5:10). This is not a judgment that determines whether a person goes to heaven or hell. Everyone who stands before the judgment seat of Christ is already saved and declared "not guilty" by God. Instead, this evaluation results in commendation and heavenly rewards for those who served the Lord faithfully.

We must all appear before
the judgment seat of Christ.
—2 Corinthians 5:10

Each of us will appear before the Lord for an evaluation to receive whatever reward is appropriate.

After you become a Christian, you no longer have to worry about God's condemnation, but you still need to be mindful of His evaluation of your life. That's why 2 Corinthians 5:10 says, "We must all appear before the judgment seat of Christ." Every Christian will stand before the judgment seat of Christ—no exceptions.

Each of us will appear before the Lord for an evaluation to receive whatever reward is appropriate. The apostle Paul wrote, "We also have as our ambition, whether at home or absent, to be pleasing to Him" (v. 9). Knowing that we will stand before Christ's evaluation, we ought to have as our one aim in life to be pleasing to God.

While we are saved by God's grace apart from our works, God rewards Christians based on our works. Our works are worthless in securing us a *place* in heaven, but they are integral in determining our *experience* in heaven.

Paul drew a distinction between works before salvation and works after salvation. This is what he said about our works before salvation: "By grace you have been saved through faith; and that not of yourselves, it is the gift of God; *not as a result of works*, so that no one may boast" (Eph. 2:8–9).

But this is what Paul said about works after salvation: "We are His workmanship, created in Christ Jesus *for good works*, which God prepared beforehand so that we would walk in them" (v. 10).

Our works are worthless in securing us a place in heaven, but they are integral in determining our experience in heaven.

Each one of us will give an account of himself to God.
—Romans 14:12

Everything we have is a trust from God: our talents, skills, gifts, and opportunities. We don't own anything—we are simply managers who are responsible to use those assets to further God's interests. At the judgment seat of Christ, we will answer the Lord's question: "What have you done with what I have entrusted to you?"

The judgment seat of Christ does not determine whether we go to heaven or hell; that was settled at our salvation. This is a judgment of rewards. And the standard by which you and I as Christians will be judged is this: Did we spend our lives on things that had eternal consequence, or did we spend our lives on things that were worthless?

Our motives really do matter before God. Proverbs 16:2 says, "All the ways of a man are clean in his own sight, but the LORD weighs the motives." You might ask, "Isn't living to earn rewards in heaven a selfish motive?"

God does not have a finite amount of resources so that if you take some from Him, He then has less. God has an inexhaustible supply of riches. When God rewards you, His net worth is not diminished one iota. In fact, when you think about it, working for rewards in heaven is a sign of what God values most in our lives, and that is faith.

Working for rewards in heaven is a sign of what God values most in our lives, and that is faith.

Blessed is a man who perseveres under trial; for once he has been approved, he will receive the crown of life which the Lord has promised to those who love Him.
—James 1:12

Those who run the race well—with the right motives—will receive what the Bible calls "crowns." Scripture speaks of at least five crowns we might receive at the judgment seat of Christ:

1. The "imperishable" crown (1 Cor. 9:25) is for those who live a disciplined, Spirit-controlled life.
2. The "crown of exultation" (1 Thess. 2:19–20) is for those who engage in evangelism and discipleship.
3. The "crown of righteousness" (2 Tim. 4:8) is bestowed on those who live obediently in anticipation of the Lord's return.
4. The "crown of life" (James 1:12; Rev. 2:10) is awarded to those who endure trials without denying Christ.
5. The "crown of glory" (1 Pet. 5:4) is reserved for those who serve Christ's church, especially pastors.

What will these "crowns" be in heaven? Some believe they are literal crowns we will wear throughout eternity. Others believe that although they may be physical crowns, these rewards are tangible benefits given at the judgment seat of Christ. These benefits include:

- *Special privileges.* Some Christians will enjoy special benefits in heaven: a special welcome by God (2 Pet. 1:11), special access to the tree of life (Rev. 2:7), and even special treatment by Christ (Luke 12:37).

- *Special positions.* Those who are faithful on earth will be rewarded with additional responsibilities in heaven.

- *Special praise.* No praise in this life will compare to the praise some will receive from Christ in the next life: "Well done, good and faithful servant!" (Matt. 25:21 NIV).

These rewards are tangible benefits given at the judgment seat of Christ.

I am the way, and the truth, and the life; no one comes to the Father but through Me.
—John 14:6

CHAPTER 9

Who Will Be in Heaven?

Some people say, "Only God can decide who is going to be in heaven." That is absolutely true. The fact is, He has already decided that. He said there is only one way to heaven, and that is through faith in Jesus Christ.

The Bible says that only those who have trusted in Christ for the forgiveness of their sins will reside in the new heaven and new earth. When we declare that faith in Christ offers the only path to heaven, we are simply repeating the requirement God established. The popular belief that all religions lead to God negates the teaching of Jesus, who declared, "I am the way, and the truth, and the life; no one comes to the Father but through Me" (John 14:6).

In Matthew 7:13–14, Jesus said that there are two roads that lead to two very different eternal destinations. He said, "Enter through the narrow gate; for the gate is wide and the way is broad that leads to destruction, and there are many who enter through it. For the gate is small and the way is narrow that leads to life, and there are few who find it."

There are two roads in life. One is a broad road. It is the highway that leads, ultimately, to hell. Jesus said most people are on that road. But Jesus said there is another road going in the opposite direction that is very narrow, and it leads to heaven.

Jesus said that there are two roads that lead to two very different eternal destinations.

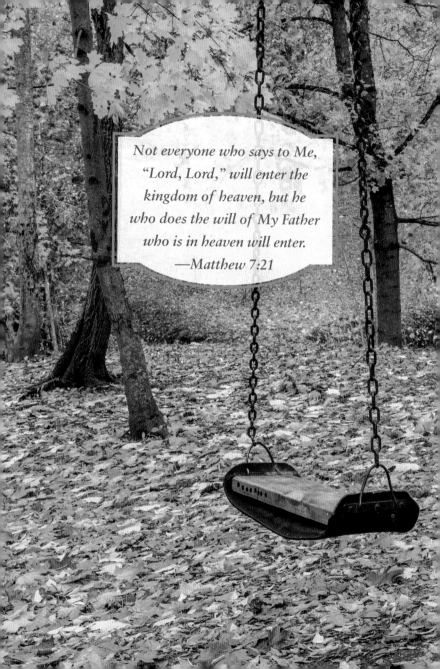

Not everyone who says to Me, "Lord, Lord," will enter the kingdom of heaven, but he who does the will of My Father who is in heaven will enter.
—Matthew 7:21

Since only God is "able to judge the thoughts and intentions of the heart" (Heb. 4:12), He alone knows who has sincerely placed his or her faith in Christ for the forgiveness of sins. People we may think should be in heaven won't be there, while many people we don't think should be in heaven will be.

Hopefully you won't be surprised about your own eternal fate. If you wait until you have passed from this life to see whether you are welcomed into God's presence, you will have waited too long. The Bible indicates many people will be surprised by their eternal destination. Although they thought they would be welcomed into heaven, God will turn them away.

Whether we acknowledge it or not, we are all sinners. Admittedly, we can always point to those who are worse than we are. We may not be as bad as we *can* be, but we are just as *bad off* as we can be. All of us have sinned (Rom. 3:23), creating an eternal gulf between God and ourselves.

The result of sin is death. "The wages of sin is death," Paul wrote in Romans 6:23. Just as physical death is the separation of our body from our spirit, spiritual death is the separation of our spirit from God. Physical death is temporary, but spiritual death is eternal. Death is God's righteous judgment on sin.

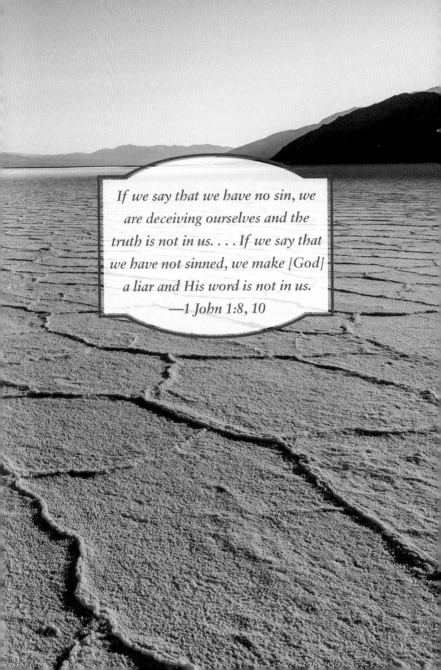

If we say that we have no sin, we are deceiving ourselves and the truth is not in us. . . . If we say that we have not sinned, we make [God] a liar and His word is not in us.
—1 John 1:8, 10

We tolerate sin because we are sinful. But God is not like we are.

Several times in the Bible, God said, "Be holy, for I am holy." That word *holy* means "different, separate, above." God is different than we are. We are sinful. God is sinless.

Many people say, "Why is God so judgmental about sin? I can overlook people's faults. Why can't God be as tolerant as I am?" The fact that you and I can overlook sin is not because we are like God; it is because we are unlike God. We tolerate sin because we are sinful. But God is not like we are. Habakkuk 1:13 says about God, "Your eyes are too pure to approve evil, and You can not look on wickedness with favor." God has zero tolerance for sin because He is holy.

Imagine you're on a road trip but don't have enough gas to get to your destination. Suddenly, a tanker stops, and the driver says, "I'm willing to give you some of my gas. May I fill your tank?" That is what Jesus does for us.

When Jesus died, He took the punishment we deserve for our sins. God is holy and cannot overlook evil. Nahum 1:3 says, "The LORD will by no means leave the guilty unpunished." Someone *has* to pay for our sins—and Jesus volunteered to do just that. When Jesus died on the cross, He took all the punishment from God that you and I deserve. Jesus also gave us His goodness, which we do not deserve. Jesus is the solution to our sin problem.

Having been justified by faith,
we have peace with God through
our Lord Jesus Christ.
—Romans 5:1

[Jesus] called a child to Himself and set him before them, and said, "Truly I say to you, unless you are converted and become like children, you will not enter the kingdom of heaven."
—Matthew 18:2–3

One of my most painful duties as a pastor is ministering to families after the loss of a child or a loved one who is mentally childlike. One question consumes their thoughts: "Are they in heaven?"

In Matthew 18:1–4, Jesus used a child to illustrate the humility necessary to receive God's forgiveness. The child Jesus selected represented all children. By His actions and words, Jesus indicated that all children (and those who are mentally childlike) are destined for heaven.

I believe we can say that our loving God welcomes children into heaven. As Abraham declared, "Shall not the Judge of all the earth deal justly?" (Gen. 18:25). We can depend on God to deal justly—and graciously—with those who are incapable of exercising faith in Christ.

God doesn't force anyone to receive His offer of forgiveness. Only those who choose to receive His gift will be granted entry into heaven (John 1:12).

Where are *you* on the road to heaven? Perhaps you are ready to open your heart to receive God's forgiveness so you can be sure that one day God will welcome you into His presence. If so, I invite you to pray the prayer on the next page. It's not a magic formula but rather a way to receive God's offer of forgiveness.

If that prayer is your heart's desire, you can be assured that you are on the road that leads to heaven.

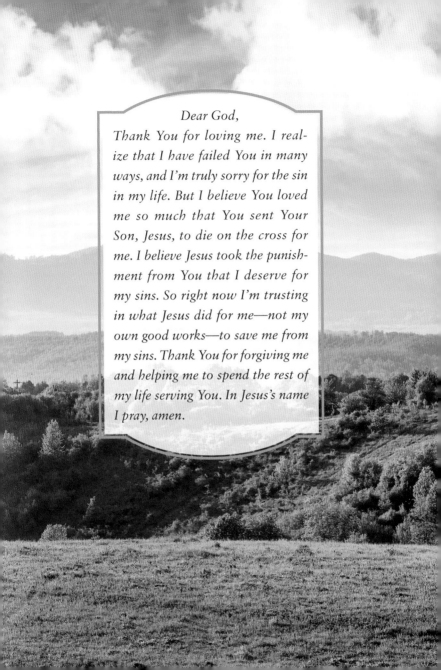

Dear God,

Thank You for loving me. I realize that I have failed You in many ways, and I'm truly sorry for the sin in my life. But I believe You loved me so much that You sent Your Son, Jesus, to die on the cross for me. I believe Jesus took the punishment from You that I deserve for my sins. So right now I'm trusting in what Jesus did for me—not my own good works—to save me from my sins. Thank You for forgiving me and helping me to spend the rest of my life serving You. In Jesus's name I pray, amen.

Faith in Christ is not just one *way to heaven—it is the* only *way to heaven.*

CHAPTER 10

How Can I Prepare for My Journey to Heaven?

Making arrangements for your journey to heaven begins with making sure you have the proper "passport." The only "document" that allows us entry into God's presence for eternity is one that is stamped "Forgiven," and it is given to us the moment we trust in Jesus Christ for our salvation. The theological term for forgiven is *justified*, which means, "to be declared righteous." Our justification before God is not based on our works but on His grace and is received by faith: "Therefore, having been justified by faith, we have peace with God through our Lord Jesus Christ" (Rom. 5:1).

Faith in Christ is not just *one* way to heaven—it is the *only* way to heaven.

How can you make sure that God will welcome you into heaven? If you wait until you die to discover your eternal destination, you will have waited too long. God doesn't want your eternal destiny to be a mystery. That's why John wrote, "These things I have written to you *who believe in the name of the Son of God, so that you may know that you have eternal life*" (1 John 5:13).

If you do not "know that you have eternal life," why not pause right now and confess to God your need for His forgiveness and express your dependence on Christ's death on the cross to save you from your sins? When you do that, you can be sure that you have made the most basic preparation necessary for your journey to heaven.

*God doesn't want
your eternal destiny
to be a mystery.*

Our citizenship is in heaven, from which also we eagerly wait for a Savior, the Lord Jesus Christ.
—Philippians 3:20

We don't know when our departure to heaven will be, so we must prepare for our trip to the next world while still living in this world. God calls us to be residents of two worlds: the next world and this world.

Make no mistake about it: our true citizenship is in heaven. Nevertheless, God has left us here as well, and He has given us certain responsibilities. We have responsibilities with the family God has entrusted to us. We have responsibilities at work. And, of course, our greatest responsibility is to be "ambassadors for Christ" (2 Cor. 5:20), urging people to be reconciled to God through faith in Jesus. We are preparing for the next world while living in this world.

As Christians we each have God-given assignments to complete during our brief stay on earth, even though we will soon be departing for our eternal home. Yet while we temporarily reside in this world, we are to guard against becoming entangled in it. We are to be thinking about and preparing for heaven, but we still have work to do here.

The Bible talks about that here/there mentality. In Hebrews 11:13, the writer said we are "strangers and exiles" on earth. In Colossians 3:2, Paul said, "Set your mind on the things above, not on the things that are on earth." But here is the irony: the more we focus on heaven, the more effective we become on earth.

The more we focus on heaven, the more effective we become on earth.

There are two reasons that Christians do not need to fear death.

First, if you are a Christian, you can be assured that you will not depart this earth one second before God's appointed time. From God's perspective, no one dies prematurely. The psalmist declared, "My times are in Your hand" (Ps. 31:15). God determines our days and numbers our years.

Second, death is a necessary transition from this world to the next world. For a Christian, death is nothing more than a transition from an inferior country to a superior one. In fact, without experiencing death, you and I could never travel to that "place called heaven."

God had a plan for Jesus's life that included the day of His birth and the day of His death. And God also has a plan for your life. In Ephesians 1:11, Paul wrote that all things have been "predestined according to His purpose who works all things after the counsel of His will."

There are no accidents in your life. No death catches God off guard. Everything, including the day of your death, is according to His will. Those who die in faith—whether they are nine or ninety—lived exactly the number of years God prescribed for them.

Your life is in God's hands. That's why no Christian needs to fear his or her departure from this world.

Your life is in God's hands.
That's why no Christian
needs to fear his or her
departure from this world.

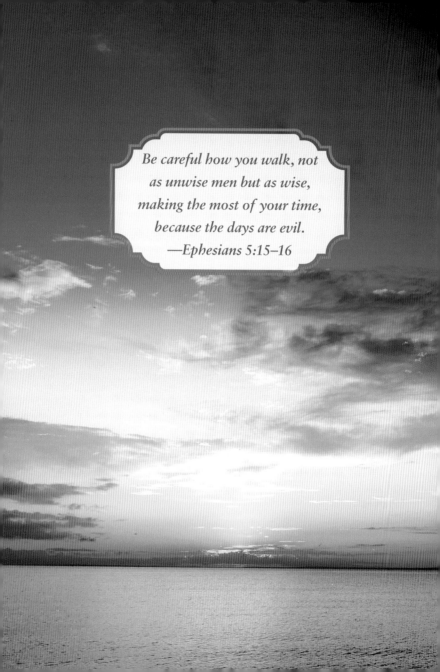

Be careful how you walk, not as unwise men but as wise, making the most of your time, because the days are evil.
—*Ephesians 5:15–16*

You can prepare for your journey to heaven by making the most of your time on earth. The apostle Paul said it this way in Ephesians 5:15–16: "Be careful how you walk, not as unwise men but as wise, making the most of your time, because the days are evil."

Here is a good exercise. Ask yourself, *What three things do I think God wants me to do before I die?* Once you get those three things in mind, then ask yourself, *As I go throughout the day, how much time do I devote to those major priorities?* Most of us spend very little time doing the things we think are the most important. That's why Paul told us to make the most of our time.

As you prepare for your journey to that "place called heaven," one of the best resolutions you can make is to rid your life of unnecessary regrets. One way to do this is to evaluate your life. Take a sheet of paper and divide it into five columns: God, family, friends, career, and finances. Under each column, write three goals you'd like to achieve in each of these areas before you die.

As you honestly evaluate your life, maybe you feel badly about mistakes you've made, opportunities you've squandered, or people you've hurt. The truth is that it is impossible to erase the past. Life has no rewind button. But with God's help, you can make some changes in your life right now that will reshape your tomorrow and your eternity.

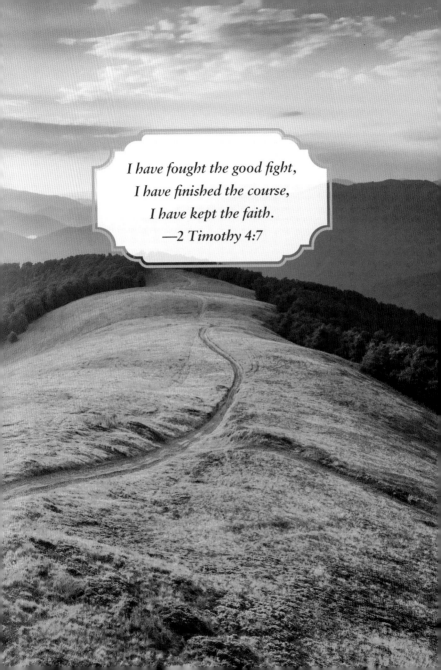

I have fought the good fight,
I have finished the course,
I have kept the faith.
—2 Timothy 4:7

*Heaven is the destination
that awaits all those who
love the Lord Jesus Christ.*

Are you ready for your journey to heaven? If you are a Christian, you need not fear the journey—especially when you consider the destination. Heaven is the destination that awaits all those who love the Lord Jesus Christ. And it is more glorious than mere words can begin to describe.

It's a place more magnificent than you could ever imagine.

It's a place where every heartache will be erased and every dream will be fulfilled.

It's a place reserved for those who have received God's forgiveness through faith in Jesus Christ.

It's a "place called heaven."

About the Author

Dr. Robert Jeffress is senior pastor of the fourteen-thousand-member First Baptist Church, Dallas, Texas, and a Fox News contributor. He is also an adjunct professor at Dallas Theological Seminary. Dr. Jeffress has made more than four thousand guest appearances on various radio and television programs and regularly appears on major mainstream media outlets such as Fox News Channel's *Fox and Friends*, *Hannity*, *Lou Dobbs Tonight*, *Varney and Co.*, and *Judge Jeanine*; ABC's *Good Morning America*; and HBO's *Real Time with Bill Maher*. Dr. Jeffress hosts a daily radio program, *Pathway to Victory*, that is heard nationwide on over one thousand stations in major markets such as Dallas–Fort Worth, New York City, Chicago, Los Angeles, Houston, Washington, DC, San Francisco, Philadelphia, and Seattle. His daily television program,

Pathway to Victory, can be seen Monday through Friday on the Trinity Broadcasting Network (TBN), every Sunday on TBN, and daily on the Hillsong Channel. *Pathway to Victory* is the second-highest rated ministry program on TBN's Sunday schedule. Dr. Jeffress's television broadcast reaches 195 countries and is on 11,295 cable and satellite systems throughout the world.

Dr. Jeffress is the author of twenty-seven books, including *Not All Roads Lead to Heaven*, *A Place Called Heaven*, *Choosing the Extraordinary Life*, *Courageous*, *Invincible*, and *Praying for America*. Dr. Jeffress led his congregation in the completion of a $135 million re-creation of its downtown campus. The project is the largest in modern church history and serves as a "spiritual oasis" covering six blocks of downtown Dallas.

Dr. Jeffress has a DMin from Southwestern Baptist Theological Seminary, a ThM from Dallas Theological Seminary, and a BS from Baylor University. In May 2010, he was awarded a Doctor of Divinity degree from Dallas Baptist University, and in June 2011, he received the Distinguished Alumnus of the Year award from Southwestern Baptist Theological Seminary.

Dr. Jeffress and his wife, Amy, have two daughters and three grandchildren.

A PLACE CALLED
HEAVEN

10 Surprising Truths about Your Eternal Home

Resources available include...

» The paperback book *A Place Called Heaven* plus "What Seven World Religions Teach about Heaven"—an easy to understand and informative companion brochure

» The complete, unedited series on DVD/CD

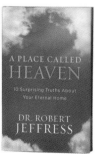

Bring Eternity to Mind Every Day

In his bestselling book *A Place Called Heaven*, Dr. Robert Jeffress opened the Scriptures to answer ten fascinating questions about heaven. Now he offers this devotional to help you think about heaven on a daily basis and put into practice the heavenly qualities of truth, honor, righteousness, purity, loveliness, character, excellence, and praise.

A PLACE CALLED
HEAVEN
FOR KIDS

Colorfully illustrated and using simple concepts and language
that children can understand, *A Place Called Heaven for Kids* gives
children peace of mind about their lost loved one as well as a
comforting, biblical picture of their forever home.

AVAILABLE WHEREVER BOOKS
AND EBOOKS ARE SOLD